My Grandpa's Stories

A. D. Ariel

Literacy Consultants
David Booth • Kathleen Corrigan

We are visiting Grandpa.

We are bringing him food.

Mama puts corn in the basket.

She puts beans in the basket.

She puts eggs in the basket.

Grandpa sees the food.

He tells us stories.

Grandpa lived on a farm
in Mexico.
We look at pictures.

We see a picture of a field.

Grandpa picked corn

in that field.

We see a picture of Grandpa.

He is a little boy.

We see a picture of a field.

Grandpa picked beans

in that field.

We see a picture of Grandpa.

He has beans.

We see beans.

Grandpa sings us a song.

The song is about baby chicks.

"The hen looks for corn.

She feeds the baby chicks,"

Grandpa sings.

We see a picture of chickens.

There were chickens
on the farm.

Grandpa looks in the basket.

He puts away the eggs.

He puts away the beans.

He puts away the corn.

"Thank you for the food," says Grandpa.

"Thank you for the song. Thank you for the pictures," we say.

We like Grandpa's song.

We like the old pictures.

We like Grandpa's stories!